THE S

100 Ways to Have a
Great Relationship

Ben Renshaw

Vermilion
LONDON

3 5 7 9 10 8 6 4

First published in 2002 by Vermilion,
an imprint of Ebury Press, Random House, 20 Vauxhall
Bridge Road, London SW1V 2SA

Random House Australia (Pty) Limited
20 Alfred Street, Milsons Point, Sydney, New South Wales
2061, Australia

Random House New Zealand Limited
18 Poland Road, Glenfield, Auckland 10, New Zealand

Random House South Africa (Pty) Limited
Endulini, 5A Jubilee Road, Parktown 2193, South Africa

The Random House Group Limited Reg. No. 954009

Papers used by Vermilion are natural, recyclable products
made from wood grown in sustainable forests

Printed and bound by Nørhaven Paperback A/S, Denmark

A CIP catalogue record for this book is available from the
British Library

ISBN 0-7126-2948-3

Acknowledgements

The Secrets is made possible due to the amazing people in my life. Thank you to my wife, Veronica, for her love, friendship and belief. Thank you to my mother, Virginia, for her wisdom and support. Thank you to my father, Peter, for his encouragement. Thank you to my sister, Sophie, for her love. Thank you to my cousin, Dave, for his creative flair and literary skills. Thank you to Robert Holden, for his constant inspiration and leadership. Thank you to Candy Constable, for her commitment. Thank you to Nick Williams, for his support. Thank you to my clients and friends at The Happiness Project. Thank you to my editor, Judith Kendra, for making it possible.

Introduction

I was a confirmed bachelor at the time. I'd had
my heart broken often enough to watch my back
carefully. However, this was different. I had met
someone and felt a commitment to making it
work that surprised even myself.

I had been introduced to Veronica through a
mutual friend. She was living in Tokyo and planning
to return to her native home in New Zealand.
Coming from London, my logic told me that it wasn't
a good idea to get involved in a long distance
relationship. However, very soon the relationship
became the number one priority in my life. I would
have done anything for it. We agreed that Veronica
would join me in London and that we'd see how it
went. Eight years later, married and expecting our

first child, my understanding of the reality of what's possible in a relationship has been transformed.

The Secrets is about how to create and sustain a loving relationship. My message is simple: a great relationship is possible, if you're willing to do what it takes. You have to work at it. You have to learn some painful lessons. You have to invest time, energy and effort. But it's worth it.

This book is based on my work with countless clients plus my own ups and downs along the way. It is a book of hope. I have witnessed pain turn into pleasure, rejection into respect, agony into acceptance and lack into love. I know that transformation is possible.

The very fact that you are reading this book leads me to believe that you are ready for new ideas, new possibilities and new beginnings that can change your experience forever.

1

Your relationship history is not your relationship destiny

Think back on your relationship history. What horrors did it include? Did you deceive your partner? Manipulate them to see only your way? Did you play power games to gain control? Believing that what happened in your past will carry into your future is not an attractive prospect.

Not for anybody.

Fortunately it doesn't have to be the case.

Commit to making new choices in your life and release those old habits that never worked for you. The new choices that you make today will yield new outcomes. This means that you can reinvent your relationship each day by making choices that truly support you.

T I P

Your future lies in the choices
that you make today

2

Divorce your parents!

'You sound just like your father,' Veronica
declared to me as I insisted that we couldn't eat
in a particular restaurant. We were hungry, on
holiday and had reached a spot that was full of
tourists and I wanted to leave. We landed up in
an argument and drove off to look for
somewhere else. After a good deal of brooding I
came to realise that similar events had occurred
with my own parents on holiday!

In my relationship workshops I ask participants: *'How many of you would like your relationship to be similar to your parents' relationship?'* The majority answer with a resounding 'No!' Yet until we become aware of our parents' influence we tend either to recreate similar habits or to rebel and try and do the opposite. Neither of these options supports a healthy relationship.

Divorcing your parents means letting go of any lingering influence that prevents you from making conscious choices in your relationship today. Identify any traits with your partner so that you can both catch them when they come up.

T I P

When you see your parents in something you do, stop and make new choices

3

Put your relationship first

I watched a programme about slavery in the 21st century. It focused on one man who worked 14–18 hours a day. He was married with two young children and he claimed that his relationship was important, but I wasn't so sure. It made me think of the saying that when you're on your death bed the last thing you're going to regret is not having spent more time at the office.

In order to have a great relationship you must make it an absolute priority. This is a challenge because our lives are so full of demands, but if your relationship comes consistently second it will suffer.

Remember: a relationship means that you are not on your own any more. You may be able to skim the surface for so long, but then your partner will want more, and rightly so. Have the courage to put your relationship first, even when you are under pressure. The sustenance that you will receive from your partner will enable you to rise to any challenge.

TIP

If it's a relationship you want,
put it first

4

Ask for help!

'I've just met the person of my dreams – help, what do I do?' We've all read this sort of letter in different agony columns and the truth is we all need help – ironically even when things are going well. The trouble is that we've all bought the independence ticket, a condition my friend Robert Holden calls being a DIP – a *Dysfunctionally Independent Person*. A DIP believes that they can survive relationships all on their own, without anyone to help them. They also think asking for help is a sign of weakness.

This is not a healthy recipe for a good relationship.

Be willing to see things differently. In truth, asking for help is a sign of strength. It bypasses unnecessary struggle and hardship. Look around at your friends and ask yourself, *'Who could best help me?'* Then ask them quickly before you change your mind.

TIP

Don't wait for a disaster before getting help from a friend

5

Recognise the 'real' you

Picture the existence of the sun. Just because you don't always see it doesn't mean that it isn't always there, shining and radiant. This is also true of you. You have a great potential, which is always there. You also have a shadow side that can cast darkness over things. In relating to yourself become aware of the existence of these two selves. The 'real you' is your *unconditioned Self* – fearless, abundant and free. The 'false you'

is your *conditioned Self* – fearful, attacking and lacking.

Since the quality of your relationship is determined by the quality of the relationship you have with yourself, remembering the 'real you' enables you to shine even when storms appear. Trust that you are a light in the world. Every time you forget you betray your original power and greatness. Every time you remember the world celebrates with you.

T I P

Look for the greatness in yourself;
you will find it

6

Rewrite your relationship story

In each of her sessions, Clare would describe another painful episode of her relationship story. She made *EastEnders'* dramas pale in comparison to her own. It was an extraordinary drama that included break-ups, reconciliations, ultimatums and thwarted dreams.

One day I asked if she would be willing to consider changing her story. Reflecting on this, she saw that recreating the same drama each

time kept her stuck and that rewriting her story
would be a good move.

How would you describe the story of your relationship? Is it a drama, comedy, tragedy, thriller,
romance or success? Does it support you? If not,
you can rewrite the script. Ask yourself, 'What
story would I like to invent with myself as the
lead character?' Discuss this with your partner to
understand how your stories may have merged
together, and how you could create a new
scenario, one that will help both of you.

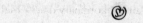

TIP
Ask yourself, 'What is the story
of my relationship right now?'
If you don't like it, change it

7

Honesty is the best policy

Dan was prone to lying. It didn't matter how big or small an issue it was, he would concoct stories that only created problems for him and his partner. He felt that honesty left him vulnerable and hurt her. I asked him to think how he would like to be treated. Would he prefer to be kept in the dark or to have the truth? Eventually he came to see that honesty could be the best policy because, as he put it, it gives people the information to make their own choices.

The key to honesty is the intention behind it. If you are honest in order to get even or to hurt your partner, it will be damaging. If you are honest in order to let go of obstacles and to create understanding, it will be worthwhile, no matter how difficult the communication. I have seen troubled relationships in which major chunks of information have been withheld, including affairs and financial matters, which once expressed enabled the couples to come to a mature choice about whether to stay together or to split up. Be willing to practise honesty in order to free yourself.

TIP

The fear of honesty is a much
greater problem than just being
honest

8

Fill up your rejection quota

I knew a man who was determined to resolve his fear of rejection. He took up a position on a street corner in New York and asked every woman who walked past for a date. The first day he got one rejection after another. He dragged himself home, licking his wounds. Day two found him back on the corner, but this time dealing with the rejection was like water off a duck's back. By day three he began to get interest and this brought on even more fear. What was he to do?

It is up to you how you see rejection. If he/she doesn't call it may mean the romance is over, or that they are simply busy. If he/she doesn't meet your every need it may mean that they don't care, or that they don't know what you want.

The next time you feel rejected ask yourself, *'What if 'rejection' is not a rejection?'* Shifting your thinking like this helps you to suspend fear and be open to new possibilities.

T I P

Look at what you make rejection mean before you jump to any conclusions

9

Become a
risk taker

Imagine yourself standing on a beach. Draw a
circle around yourself in the sand. Now take a
step out of the circle. You have just stepped out
of your comfort zone.
We live in our own cocoon of familiarity which
protects us from our perceived fears and dislikes.
However, it can become a prison in which we
can get stuck. We become afraid to take risks.
We play safe and limit the potential for growth
and opportunity in our lives.

Decide to become a risk taker. This doesn't mean
that you have to take huge leaps immediately.
You can follow the wise Chinese saying, *'The
journey of a thousand miles starts with a single
step.'* Ask yourself, *'What would be a risk for me
today?'* For example; To communicate more? To
love more? To give more? To receive more?
Commit to moving out of your comfort zone in
order to live more fully.

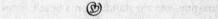

T I P
Start taking risks,
it's fun

10

Be honest about your desire for a relationship

Simon had been single for some time when he came to see me. As we discussed his situation it became more and more clear to him that his deepest desire was to be loved. Staying single had been a protection that in the end was starving him.

We all protect ourselves from getting hurt in one form or another. However, until we get off the shelf and put ourselves in the window it will be virtually impossible either to create a relationship or to enhance the one we are already in.

Stop playing safe. Admit your desire for a relationship and recognise that although it's a risk, it's one that's worth taking. Being honest about your desire enables you to move in the direction that you want to go.

T I P

In order to get where you want,
admit it

11

Get comfortable with the words 'I love you'

A client came to see me, exasperated. She had been going out with her boyfriend for over a year, and had been waiting to hear the 'L' word. She was still waiting. Sound familiar?

Often one of the biggest hurdles in a relationship is either to say, 'I love you', or to hear 'I love you'. Since the majority of people have had their heart broken at least once, it's safe to say that it gets harder to express love. Ask yourself, *'What is my block to expressing love?'* For example, you may have it wired up with the fear of commitment, or of feeling trapped and obligated, which then causes you to hold back. Recognise that having the courage to express love again, and mean it, creates a new beginning for a relationship.

TIP

The greatest way to mend a broken
heart is to love again

12

Know what you want – but don't be attached to what he or she looks like

When Dave came to see me he insisted that his ideal type was a 'tall, thin, blonde'. However, when we reviewed his relationship history we came to see that his relationships with his 'ideal type' had never worked out. In fact, Dave ended up marrying someone bearing no resemblance to

the fantasy figure he had longed for. He finally
realised that the qualities he wanted had no
connection to physical appearance.

Becoming too invested in what you think you
want can be a big deception. Getting too
attached to a particular image is like wearing
blinkers that prevent you from having a wider
vision. Be willing to be surprised. Make yourself
available for new experiences.

TIP

Be willing to be amazed!

13

No expectations

I coached a couple that were keeping score.
Constantly. John expected dinner on the table
when he got home. Ruth expected the DIY jobs
to be done at the weekend. John expected sex
every Saturday night. Ruth expected him to
handle the finances. Neither was winning.

When you have an expectation that something
'should' be a certain way, you're setting yourself
up for disappointment. Waiting for what you
believe is owed to you, and getting upset if it
doesn't appear, will only lead to more
disappointment.

Remember that once a wish becomes an
expectation you are treading on thin ice.
Holding on to expectations is the surest way to
prevent your partner from meeting your needs,
and if they do they will probably feel resentful.
Expectations bring nothing but harm because
they can never be fulfilled.

TIP

Confess your expectations for the
purpose of giving them up

14

You can be light and deep at the same time

I used to love deep conversations. The heavier the better. It fulfilled my belief that relationships were a serious business. If a person made light of a situation I usually perceived them as superficial. When I met Veronica she had a slightly different outlook. Growing up in a family of eight children, which included four brothers, she didn't have much chance to be too heavy for too long. She brought this lightness into our relationship. I took some time to get used to it but I learnt that it was possible to be light and deep at the same time.

This secret can be a lifesaver. It enables you to retain a sense of perspective when difficult issues arise and helps to keep communication open. Often the turning point in a conflict is when you're able to laugh. It can bring a new way of seeing a situation, a fresh thought, and a leap of faith which can change your relationship forever.

TIP

laughter is a great medicine

15

Catch your partner getting things right

Last summer I was sitting in a restaurant, eavesdropping. The couple on the next table were having a heart to heart. She was enthusiastically talking about a work opportunity. To everything she said he pointed out what she was doing wrong. Within minutes she was deflated. Are you better at catching your partner getting things wrong, or getting things right? Do you focus on their failures, or their successes?

One of the greatest gifts that you can give your partner is to spot their strengths. It brings out the best in them and reinforces their confidence. All it takes is one person to genuinely believe in your ability and you can take on the world. Be this person for your partner. Hold up a mirror that shows them how great they already are. This gives them the freedom to take risks, to shine and to excel. Remember that what you give your partner you also give yourself.

TIP

Recognise and celebrate
your partner's successes,
no matter how small

16

It's a numbers game

At a recent workshop a participant told how she had been single for several years before deciding to re-enter the dating game. She joined a variety of agencies and went out on more than thirty dates. No one was suitable. She stopped looking and then happened to meet up with a man she already knew, but had never considered as a possible partner. She is now in a great relationship with him.

Welcome to the real lottery – the relationship game. Whenever someone claims that they can never meet anyone right, that all the good guys are taken, I gently remind them that we live in a world of six billion people. They only need one! The key is to stay open to meeting people since out of 'x' amount of 'possible partners' you are going to find one. The truth is that it could happen at any time, just be open.

T I P

Be prepared to say 'yes' to going out and meeting people. You have to buy a ticket to play the game

17

Stop waiting, start living

Have you ever caught yourself waiting for things to get good in your relationship before you fully commit? Have you ever waited for your partner to meet your needs before making a move to meet theirs? Welcome to *The WAIT Problem*, which is a game we play when we're afraid of taking a risk, of fully committing and of taking responsibility for the relationship in our lives.

Stop waiting and be decisive. Your willingness to make new choices opens the door to new possibilities. For example, if you are waiting for love, choose to become loving. If you are waiting for understanding, choose to understand. If you are waiting for affection, choose to be affectionate. Your decision to choose the very things that you most want brings them into your life.

TIP

Take responsibility for what you want to see happen

18

Wear your
partner's shoes

*'He/she is amazing. They understand me so well.
It's as if they can read my mind.'* Would you like
your partner to say that about you? If so, it's
time to develop the quality of empathy, that is
to place yourself as fully as you can in your
partner's shoes. Start by imagining seeing the
world as if through their eyes, feeling the world
as if through their emotions and touching the

world as if through their body. Projecting into the world of your partner is an amazing experience.

Developing empathy is not an intellectual exercise. It has to come from your heart and soul. Listen with the intent to understand. This will provide the glue that binds your relationship.

TIP

Wear your partner's shoes;
you'll find they fit

19

You can have your passion cake – and eat it

Your heart is on fire. Adrenaline is coursing through your blood. Every word and touch is ecstatic. It's what you yearn for – passion.

However, passion is not a constant in a relationship. It comes and goes. If you notice that it's been missing for some time, decide to reconnect to your original passion. The failure to do so can mean that your relationship hits a 'dead zone', characterised by a breakdown in communication and loss of sexual activity and intimacy.

Remember what arouses your passion. For instance; a romantic dinner, a stroll in the countryside, hearing great music or seeing beautiful art. Share something together that reconnects you again.

TIP

You can always bake another cake
once you know the ingredients

20

Make sure your ladder is leaning against the right wall

'I saw him at the bar. He looked gorgeous. My friend persuaded me to talk to him. We landed up going out for nearly six months. Unfortunately it was a disaster because he was completely unsuitable but I felt guilty about ending it.' Sound familiar?

If you're looking for a relationship it's important to know what qualities, characteristics and behaviours you would like it to have. Otherwise you may find yourself working hard at relationships without having worked out what a successful one truly is.

I often coach people who go from one relationship to another only to experience the same thing. It is only when they stop to re-evaluate their priorities that things begin to change. For example, if communication is important to you and you attract someone to whom it isn't important, learn to say 'no' and walk away. Having the courage to say 'no' is a crucial part of breaking old habits. It is also the first step in saying 'yes' to what you really want.

TIP

Decide what's important to you in a relationship and stick to it

21

Forgive fast

A client recounted their experience of the power
of forgiveness. 'My heart was broken. My
girlfriend had left me for a close friend.
I was consumed with anger, jealousy and a desire
for revenge. I tried to get my own back, but to no
avail. It hurt even more. I resisted forgiveness;
it seemed impossible. Eventually I became willing
to forgive. The pain lessened. I knew that I had
fully forgiven them when one day I felt free again.'

The way out of any grievance, wound, pain or hurt is forgiveness. To forgive is to give forth your love and to receive peace in return. Often the obstacle to forgiveness is feeling that you're letting somebody off the hook. The trouble with holding on to upsets is that you're the one that suffers. Your ex-partner may be happily getting on with their life, but you're still waiting. There is a difference between forgiving someone and condoning their behaviour. Forgiveness is not logical. It bypasses the rational mind and goes straight to the heart.

T I P

The key to forgiveness
is your willingness

22

Take responsibility for all your experiences

Bob shared with me what is a common scenario in many relationships. He claimed that his partner wouldn't stop going on at him. In fact he had resorted to calling her the 'nag'. Apparently she 'nagged' him to spend time together, she 'nagged' him to get DIY jobs done and she 'nagged' him to dress in a particular way. What

Bob didn't realise was that he was playing out a 'victim role' by conveniently blaming his partner.

The trouble with blame is that it keeps you stuck in negative habits and prevents you from making changes for the better. It is important to learn to recognise when you are blaming. As soon as you hear yourself thinking or saying things such as: 'It's your fault', or 'If only you would behave differently', then admit that you're doing it. Be prepared to take responsibility for your experience. Responsibility means the ability to choose your response. Remind yourself that you're not a victim and that it's up to you whether your relationship supports or hinders you.

TIP

Taking responsibility liberates you

23

Close the door on past lovers

Are you holding on to old letters and photographs from past lovers? If so, would you be prepared to let them go? It is amazing how powerful the grip can be when holding on to memories. The trouble is that they can colour your present outlook and prevent you from fulfilling your relationship potential. For instance, you may push people away, even if you secretly long for intimacy, because you were hurt in the past. You may compare your partner with a past lover in ways they can never live up to.

Closure is what most people are lacking, and the key to closure is taking time to say goodbye. Enable yourself to let go by writing letters to past lovers, and then burn them or throw them away. This gives you the chance to communicate any unexpressed thoughts and feelings, and to let go of old attachments.

TIP

As you let go of your past you open to a whole new future

24

A relationship happens when you least expect it!

If you are single, be warned! You never know when the right person is going to show up in your life. When I met my wife Veronica I certainly wasn't looking for a relationship. I was enjoying bachelorhood and a committed relationship was not on the cards – little did I know!

You hear over and over again how somebody met their partner when they were least expecting it. You are at your most attractive when you are not desperately seeking. Nobody wants to go out with a desperate person. Focus on yourself and your life. Be happy, do what you love, keep healthy and have fun. This means that you take responsibility for yourself and your life and that you do not rely on a relationship to make everything okay.

TIP

Get on with your life
and live fully

25

Keep your running shoes by the door

I woke up in a sweat. I had to get out. I felt trapped. Veronica turned to me and said, 'Your running shoes are by the door; the choice is yours'. A look of panic came over my face, and then relief. I realised that I did have a choice to come and go. Remembering this prevents you from holding your partner responsible for your choices.

You are not in a relationship against your will.
If it feels like that, wake up. You are not a victim.
Because we live in a world where we put a high
price on our personal freedom a relationship is
often associated with a loss of independence.
This is a false notion, which prevents many
people from getting involved. Be willing to
change your mind. A relationship is not a death
sentence. It is a life sentenced to greater
freedom, happiness and joy.

TIP

Being in a relationship is a choice
that you make from moment to
moment

26

Remember how great you are

My godson is nearing nine years old. When I see him he tells me about all the great things he gets up to. He shows me his schoolwork and drawings with pride. He tells me about his great friends. I hope that when he grows up he won't forget how great he is.

Unless you are encouraged to remember how great you are it can become a distant memory. Be careful of hanging your self-image on your partner. You don't want it to become a heavy weight around their neck. It is up to you to believe in yourself. Your partner already sees how great you are otherwise they wouldn't be with you. Ask yourself, *'What are the special qualities that make me irresistible?'* Whether it's your sense of humour, your big heart or your ability to listen, never forget how great you are.

The key to unlocking your self-worth lies in your own hands

27

Your partner is a mirror reflecting back your own mind

Susan claimed that she wanted her partner to move in. Barry was reluctant and kept delaying the decision. She was getting increasingly irritated until she realised that in fact she was ambivalent about him moving in.

There is a great temptation to blame your partner for things that you yourself are unhappy about. In truth your partner is showing you an aspect of yourself that you don't want to see. For instance, if they show indecisiveness you must be the first to get things clear. Then they will have to make a move.

Your willingness to take responsibility for your own experience ensures that whatever happens you will move forward in your life with greater certainty.

TIP

Take a stand about what you
want to see

28

Understand polarities

I worked with a couple that struggled with financial issues. One day the bloke would worry about not having enough money whereas his girlfriend would spend freely. The next she was anxiously saving the pennies whereas he was reassuring her that everything was okay.

There is a habit in relationships to take extreme opposite positions. These polarities can tear you apart, giving rise to misunderstandings, as if you live in different worlds. Recognise that these very same polarities are valuable if they are understood. Each person can gain tremendous insight from the other if they are prepared to listen and learn. Ask yourself, *'How can I benefit from my partner's position?'* Once you understand the polarities it enables you to find a middle path that you can walk together.

TIP

Be willing to move from extreme positions to a middle way

29

100%

Communication

Only seven per cent of communication is through the words we speak. What are you communicating in other ways?

Great communication equals a great relationship. Without good communication understanding breaks down, trust issues arise, anger brews and hurt ensues.

Commit to communicating fully in your relationship. Agree that no matter how difficult it is you will continue to work on it together. This provides the emotional safety in which you can learn and grow. One couple I worked with shared that after twelve years of marriage they had fallen into a habit of not looking at each other when they spoke together. They realised that it had caused them to become distant. They decided to renew eye contact when in conversation, and this went a long way to restoring their closeness.

The essence of communication is to put your heart and soul into it. Express yourself fully, listen closely and be willing to keep going until you have mutual understanding.

Have the courage to
communicate fully

30

Let's talk about sex

Woody Allen once said that 'sex without love is an empty experience, but as empty experiences go, it's pretty good'. In modern living sex without love has become a norm. Men tend to believe that they can satisfy their sexual needs without becoming emotionally involved and women may use it to fill gaps in their lives. This behaviour can be hard to give up when we want to create an intimate relationship. The starting point is to get good at talking about sex in order to gain a deeper understanding within your relationship.

Recognise that in a monogamous relationship sex plays a different role than in the dating game. I often hear couples saying that they are too tired to have sex; the demands of work or a family take over. Talking about sex helps to resolve any sexual dilemmas and to keep the romance and passion alive.

T I P

Make sufficient time to talk about and have sex

31

If the bed squeaks,
fix it!

How often do you procrastinate over little jobs,
putting them off until it's nearly too late? This is
not a good strategy to employ in a relationship.
For instance, maybe you know that there is a
communication you need to make, but you keep
delaying it. Perhaps you are aware that there is
an action that you need to take, but you
postpone it. Continuing this behaviour means
that little issues may turn into big concerns.

Use the 'carrot and stick technique' in order to stop procrastinating. Think about the potential pain that you'll get if you continue to procrastinate and the pleasure that you'll receive if you don't. For example, a couple needed to discuss the husband's new job offer but they kept putting it off. Eventually they recognised that the 'carrot' of better prospects and better pay outweighed the 'stick' of moving home.

Ask yourself, *'What am I procrastinating about right now?'* Find out and do it.

T I P

Stop procrastinating and do it now

32

There's always a flip side to the coin

I worked with a couple who found it impossible
to agree. He would claim that they didn't have
enough money, whilst she stated that they did.
She would argue that he didn't make her a priority,
when he believed that he did. This highlights one
of the biggest issues that colours a relationship –
wanting to be right over being happy.

Ask yourself, 'Would I rather be right or happy?'
You may well want both, but given the choice,

which would you go for? The stubborn side of
your personality will want to be right, whatever
the cost. However, you will find that it's usually
a high price that you pay, including constant
arguing, high tension and a lack of intimacy.

Being willing to be happy means that you are
prepared to be flexible, to soften your position
and to recognise that there is always another
way of seeing a situation. Choose happiness and
watch your smiles grow.

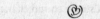

TIP

Choose happiness before
anything else

33

Remember: you're on the same side

It's World War Three. The guns go off and you start attacking each other, left, right and centre. At these moments it's easy to forget that in truth you're not enemies, you're not out to ruin each other's lives and that in fact you're both on the same side.

It is vital to be able to handle these moments of attack in constructive ways. If you have a tendency to go to war, discuss it when you're not fighting. It's usually the result of a lack of trust. Maybe you were wounded in the past and therefore you're protecting yourself now. Perhaps you saw your parents constantly fighting and it became your role model for a relationship.

Clarify what you're bringing to the table. Is it peace or war, conflict or resolution? Decide that wars may happen, but the ability to resolve them quickly is essential for your health and happiness.

TIP
On the other side of war are greater love, greater understanding and greater trust

34

Attitude is everything

Take a look at the following statement and register what you see:

LOVEISNOWHERE

Did you read: 'love is nowhere' or 'love is now here'? The law of perception says be careful what you look for because you'll find it! If you look for love you will find it and if you look for an obstacle to love you'll find that too.

Check to see if you lean towards seeing the glass as half full or half empty. Do you perceive your relationship as a blessing, or a block? Do you see the gifts that your partner has to offer, or the difficulties?

We can all fall into the trap of tunnel vision, seeing only as far as our attitude allows us. Let me ask you this, *'Who is right, the pessimist or the optimist?'* They both are! Remember: your attitude has a major impact on your relationship. It will determine whether you rise and shine each day or rise and whine.

TIP

Spring clean your attitude
to freshen up your life

35

Put your worst foot forward

We were in India. It was the first time that I had spent extended time with Veronica. Now those of you who have visited this extraordinary country will be aware that you have to be prepared for anything. Within two days of meeting her I had been hit with 'Delhi belly'. It is hard to create a good impression when you are running to the toilet every five minutes!

The blessing in disguise is that when you put your worst foot forward you're able to bypass many of the niceties that keep a relationship in a state of pretence. It helps you to find out how compatible you really are. On the television programme *Perfect Match* which I presented, one couple went camping within the first week of being together. The trip turned into a nightmare as the girl struggled to cope with the demands of a different environment. It helped to accelerate their awareness that the relationship had no future. The quicker you let someone know the 'real' you, the quicker you will discover what works.

TIP
Showing all your colours breaks
through false images

36

Make all your feelings OK

'Oh my God I'm having a feeling. What shall I do?' The classic response of an Englishman trying to keep a stiff upper lip! The one guarantee in a relationship is that you will have feelings. In fact you are going to have a huge bag of them, ranging from intense joy, passion and love to anger, anxiety and frustration. Make all your feelings okay by learning to respond to them in the following ways:

- Listen to your feelings, they are telling you something. Ask yourself *What is this feeling*

telling me?' Listen to your inner voice and
follow the message.

- Feel your feelings. What you can feel, you can heal. What you block gets stuck.

- See all feelings as an opportunity for growth. There is no such thing as a negative feeling. Accept them and move on.

- Talk to your feelings as if they were good friends. Get to know them intimately so that you can read the signs.

Developing your emotional intelligence enables you to have the peace and happiness you seek.

T I P

Within a feeling is a gift waiting to
be unwrapped

37

Unless you are happy with yourself, you will not be happy with who you are with

There is a story of a man who searched all over the world to find a relationship that would make him happy. The last I heard he was still searching!

One of the greatest lessons that I have learnt about happiness, as co-director of The Happiness Project, is that you are responsible for your own happiness. A great relationship can encourage you to be happy, money can put a smile on your face and achievement can help you to feel successful, but nothing in itself can make you happy. Only you have the ability to do that.

The way to become happy with yourself is through self-acceptance. Self-acceptance is the magical power that wipes away self-doubt, self-judgement and self-attack. Imagine how your life would be if you practised self-acceptance. Make this commitment and watch your life transform.

TIP

Being happy with yourself is a choice that you can make

38

Get infected by the love virus

There is one virus that should come with a government health warning – love. It can seriously improve your health! Love heals old wounds. Love restores hope. Love dissolves defences. Love makes all things possible. Are you sure that you are getting enough love in your life? If not, decide to open yourself to love again. Make love an invitation that it cannot refuse.

When you put love first, before everything, it transforms your relationship. Love strips away any illusions, allowing the essence of your relationship to be revealed. It is your power, your true purpose. There is no higher place on Earth than a loving relationship. It is a sacred space that costs nothing, requires no long haul travel and leaves no jet lag.

TIP

Make love more important
than anything

39

Relationships are a cool place to be

Make friends with relationships. Previous
heartbreaks often lead us to construct a story in
which we claim that we're okay on our own and
that we don't need a relationship. However,
don't deny what a great gift a relationship is.
Nothing can replace having a partner who loves
and values you. Don't listen to your single friends
if they try to persuade you to forget about
creating a relationship.

A good starting point for developing a great relationship is to start believing in them. Since what you believe is what you get, opening yourself to the idea that relationships are a cool place to be allows it to become your reality. There is no substitute for the companionship and intimacy that comes from having a fulfilling relationship.

Become a Number 1 fan of relationships

40

Commitment sets you free

Be honest with yourself: are you afraid of commitment? Do you find that as soon as you are in a relationship, you are looking for an exit route? Do you equate commitment with unwelcome responsibility and obligation? If so, it's time to change your understanding.

Real commitment sets you free as it liberates you from your fears. Until you commit you do not know the truth about a relationship.

Sitting on the fence and being non-committal keeps you stuck. The way to break through commitment phobia is to have the courage to face it. Be willing to communicate your fear to your partner for the purpose of letting it go. You may be surprised to find that they have the same fear. Remember that on the other side of fear is freedom. Your reality will shift as your fears lessen, enabling you to make the most of your relationship.

T I P

Commitment is the choice to give
yourself fully in a relationship

41

It's big to say 'I'm sorry'

We all make mistakes. Are you willing genuinely to apologise when you have caused an upset? Notice the voice inside your head that would rather be right about your position than have peace. It strings you along with such lines as: 'They should apologise first', 'Why do I always have to say sorry?' 'It's not all my fault'. There may be some truth in these statements; however, you will not find what you are looking for through being stubborn and superior.

It takes large amounts of humility to survive a relationship. You need to be prepared to get on your knees and admit that you don't have all the answers, that you are always learning and that you are willing to find a better way. A true apology is a sign of your bigness and strength. You will be respected for it.

TIP

A genuine apology is a loving act

42

The grass
is greener
on your side

I spent several years searching for the greenest
grass. I changed careers, lived in different
countries and had a variety of relationships, but I
didn't find it!

We live in a world that promotes more, better
and best as the greenest grass. It encourages us

to search but never to find. It is like being a hamster on a running wheel that is unable to get off.

The solution is to recognise that the greenest grass is appreciating what you already have. There is a saying that *'gratitude is the shortest shortcut to happiness'*. Your ability to be genuinely grateful for your relationship today, your job today, your home today and your family today, means that you can be fully present to your life. This enables you to benefit from the multitude of gifts waiting for you to unwrap.

TIP

Count your blessings today

43

One plus one equals infinite possibility

Think partnership. You're so much stronger as a team, pulling together, than functioning on your own. In this age of the overly independent person you need to give up your 'me' mentality and start thinking in terms of 'we'. This creates a condition known as synergy, which means that the whole is greater than the sum of its parts.

In other words you create so much more in a relationship. You enjoy so much more as a partnership.

In order to make the most of the infinite possibilities generated by a relationship, stay open, trusting and giving. Recognise the gifts that your partner brings you. Value their insights, ideas and observations because there will be gems for you to receive. Synergy is an exciting business. It releases a well of creativity that takes you into unknown pastures, giving rise to new initiatives and ways of living.

TIP

Great minds don't think alike –
welcome your partner's ideas

44

Mission possible

How much baggage are you carrying from your past relationships? How many fears are you carrying about the future? How many issues do you have to resolve right now?

A relationship can appear an impossible feat, but remember: however large the obstacle, however big the block, however threatening the feeling, there is always light at the end of the tunnel.

You may not know the final destination, but there is always a solution.

The philosopher Robert Schuller called this attitude 'possibility thinking'. A possibility thinker turns straw into gold, creates something out of nothing. When it appears that the odds are stacked against you, ask yourself, *'What is possible here?'* Get creative in your thinking. You cannot solve a problem with the same type of thinking that created it. Be willing to play with different options until you feel an inner light bulb switch on that shows you the way ahead.

T I P

Become a 'possibility thinker'

45

No more judgement days

In the early stages of a relationship your partner can do no wrong. You see them with eyes of unconditional love. How long does it last - a day, a week, maybe several months? There comes a point when they fall off their pedestal and you're left with the harsh reality - that they're a regular human being and susceptible to all the same quirks as everybody else. However, it's vital not to use this as evidence against them.

I have watched many relationships die due to
the amount of judgement that was flying back
and forth. Recognise that judgement masks your
own insecurities and lack of understanding. It's
also a projection of the judgements that you
have about yourself. How do you judge your
partner? Do you perceive them as being too
weak, too needy, too lazy, or not good enough?
If so, be open to spot the truth about them.
Since judgement blocks love, your willingness to
relinquish it enables you to reconnect with the
original potential of your relationship.

T I P

No amount of judgement will bring
what you want

46

Give up guilt

Guilt – less of an emotion, more of a way of life!
If you're taking a guilt trip in your relationship,
beware. It takes away spontaneity, playfulness
and pleasure and gives rise to anxiety, stress and
conflict.

The type of guilt I'm referring to is like a low
current of electricity running through your body.
It often stems from childhood, particularly if you
felt that you couldn't please your parents or live
up to their expectations. As an adult you run
the same story with your partner. You fear that

you're not going to please them, your behaviour becomes subservient, you spend your life apologising and none of it's rational.

Remember: guilt is the mafia of the mind. It's a protection racket that you sell yourself. The storyline is that as long as you feel guilty it's okay, your partner cannot make you feel bad because you already feel so terrible! But guilt is not a solution. Give it up and reclaim your innocence and joy.

TIP
Forgiving yourself is your exit route out of guilt

47

There's more to love than meets the eye

Have you ever fallen in love only to enter a turbulent storm? This is because love activates the release of unresolved issues, such as fear and hurt, for the purpose of healing them. However, when you're in the eye of the storm it doesn't feel like a blessing. At these times it's vital to remind yourself that whatever is getting stirred up is on its way out.

Picture a glass with mud in the bottom. If you pour water into the glass it stirs up the mud,

creating a murky liquid. If you continue to pour
in water, the mud overflows and you're left with
a clear glass. In this analogy the glass represents a
relationship, the water is love and the mud is
any unresolved issues.

Recognise that love heals. It flushes out any
limiting factors that may block your relationship.
By remaining focused on love, clarity will emerge.

T I P

Whenever you drift from love
you will return to it because
love is your natural state

48

Be your own
best friend

There was a time in my life when I didn't enjoy
being in my own company. A turning point came
when I locked myself in my home for a weekend,
drew the curtains, turned off the phone and
faced my demons. Every negative image about
myself flashed through my mind. It was the
longest 48 hours of my life, but I came out the
other side realising that I wasn't so bad after all.

We often fear the worst about ourselves without it holding any truth. Learn to become your own best friend so that a relationship is a great bonus. Unless you enjoy spending time in your own company you will find it difficult to let somebody else do so. Treat yourself as you would like to be treated. Show yourself respect and understanding and focus on the qualities that you like about yourself. This will enable you to feel good about yourself and to let other people in.

TIP

Value yourself because
you're worth it

49

Hold your nerve when the going gets tough

Stressed out? Anxious? Pressured? What do you do when a relationship hits rocky ground? Fight or flight? I used to go for the flight response. If a relationship seemed not to be working I had already packed my bags. Separation appeared the answer. One day it hit me; there must be a better way.

In truth it is far more rewarding to hang in there when the going gets tough. Remind yourself that there is calm after a storm. Tell yourself *even this will pass* when you feel that you're at the point of no return. It's funny how when things go well you can be waiting for the fall, but when you're on a downward spiral, it feels as if it will go on forever. Remember: there is always a light at the end of the tunnel. Having contrast and ups and downs adds to the richness of being together.

TIP

When in the eye of the storm tell yourself *even this will pass*

50

Get sane before reacting

How often have you said '*I've had enough, I'm leaving*'? How often do you fly off the handle and say something that you later regret? A valuable aid is to learn to hold your tongue long enough not to make an upset worse.

It's natural for emotions to run high in a relationship. Think about how difficult it can be to handle your own stress, let alone the stress of

your partner! Develop some strategies that
enable you to cool down. For instance, count to
ten before saying something in the heat of the
moment. Take five long, deep breaths and empty
your mind. Go for a walk to cool off or go and
have a work out in the gym. Talk to a friend to
get an objective viewpoint before responding.
Write down how you are feeling to get it out of
your system. The effort you make to resume
sanity will not go unappreciated.

TIP

Discover what makes you sane
and use it

51

There is no special prize for martyrdom

'I'll do the shopping. I'll do the cleaning. I'll pay the bills. I'll shoulder the blame for any disputes.' The cries of a martyr. It looks impressive. It sounds noble. But ultimately there will be no happy ending.

Do you ever sacrifice yourself in the name of your relationship? If so, recognise that you are treading on thin ice. With martyrdom there are no winners. Everyone loses because sacrifice is not a real solution. It can provide a temporary plaster that covers up surface scratches, but eventually any deep wounds will leave their mark.

The way out of martyrdom is to recognise how you are being a martyr. Ask yourself, *'Where am I in sacrifice at the moment?'* Then make another choice. Choose to have your needs met. Choose to balance responsibilities. Choose to receive the love, support and joy that are rightly yours.

TIP

Your happiness is a gift for your partner

52

Give up control

Are you a 'control freak'? To find out read on:

1. Do you strive to keep your independence?
2. Do you get angry and blame your partner when you don't get your needs met?
3. Do you dominate your partner by making them fear you?
4. Do you have unpredictable moods?
5. Do you ask for help only when you are ill, and then reluctantly?
6. Do you attempt to convince your partner of how they 'should' think and feel?

If you answered 'yes' to three or more, you

exhibit the symptoms of an excessive need to be in control.

Learn to recognise that control is fear. It's the result of old pain, old wounds and old heartbreak. We try and protect ourselves through control but it doesn't work. It only brings more suffering as it gives rise to power struggles and disillusionment. Be prepared to admit where you are controlling and be willing to let go of your fear. Ask yourself, *'If I had no fear what would I do differently?'* Replacing control with greater trust makes you available for the highest possible outcome in your relationship.

T I P

When you relax you transform
everything

53

Don't be surprised if the shit hits the fan on holiday

You've booked your dream holiday together. Expectations are running high. For most of the year you've been sweating it out in the office, catching time together when you can. Now you are thrown together in the deep end. He wants to go hiking; she wants to lie on the beach.

He wants to watch football at night; she wants a romantic dinner.

The key is to communicate. Discuss beforehand what you want on your holiday. Find a way of meeting each other's needs. Recognise that upsets may well occur, particularly as you de-stress from your normal life. Keep a sense of perspective. You will look back and laugh about what happened.

TIP

Take the pressure off
whilst on holiday by giving
each other a break

54

Beware the familiarity zone

Do you remember the early days of your relationship when every moment spent together was like eating a gourmet meal? You savoured your time together and the experiences that you shared. Then something changed. Familiarity crept in. Like a packaged meal your relationship became predictable and lost its unique taste.

Stop taking your relationship for granted. Pull yourself out of the familiarity zone by picturing your relationship as if through new eyes. Each day ask yourself, *'What do I truly appreciate about my relationship?'* Since what you appreciate appreciates in value, your relationship will go from strength to strength.

TIP

Look for what's precious in your relationship

55

Be honest about your fantasies

He/she's the one that you want. He/she's going to fulfil your every desire. The only trouble is this 'he/she' doesn't have a name, number or address. He/she is a fantasy living in your head! Coming to terms with your fantasies is important, and it's what you do with them that makes the difference. Be careful of comparing your partner to the fantasy, or of holding back in your relationship, waiting for the fantasy to materialise. Recognise that a fantasy is exactly that, an illusion in your own mind.

Establish an understanding in your relationship that enables you to be honest about your fantasies. Be clear that the purpose of talking about a fantasy is to let it go. Once expressed it can shift. This will come as a considerable relief and enable you to become closer.

TIP

A fantasy is a bubble
that you can burst

56

Mark your territory with sturdy fences

See if you relate to the following scenes:

- Your partner goes to play tennis. They tell you that they'll be home in two hours. Three hours later you are still waiting.

- Your partner goes shopping. You have an agreed budget. They arrive home with enough bags to fill the spare room.

- You go to a party. Your partner spends the evening flirting with other people.

These events occur because you have not created strong boundaries. A boundary is an agreement about what works and what doesn't work within your relationship. For instance, having clear boundaries would mean that your partner comes home at the agreed time, or calls to check if it's okay to change the arrangement. Your partner would spend only the agreed budget, and your partner would show you respect in their interaction with others. Establishing clear boundaries enables you to ask for what you want and to have your needs met. It creates the necessary safety and trust for your relationship to flourish.

T I P

Decide on your boundaries and
stick to them

57

Money matters

Can money buy you happiness? No, but at least you can arrive at your problems in style! There's no doubt that when money matters are sorted out it makes life easier. In fact, financial issues are one of the most common causes of relationship breakdown. This is because money acts as a magnifying glass which highlights problems, fears, power struggles and disputes.

I had one client whose relationship with a divorcee broke down because she was concerned that her maintenance would be stopped.

Another client felt controlled by her partner because he pulled the financial strings, and in another case a client felt inadequate in his relationship because he didn't believe that he had enough money.

Whatever your financial status it's important to make agreements together. Are you going to share finances or keep them separate? Are you going to have a joint budget or not? Whatever you choose, make sure that you are happy with it. Review your position regularly in order to prevent money being used as a hidden weapon.

TIP

Make money your friend
by looking after it well

58

If children are in the equation, work out your formula together

Whether you have children, or you are thinking of having children, make sure that you are unified in your outlook and approach. It is common for conflict to emerge when people's parenting styles clash. One person may be more disciplined, the other more flexible.

One person might insist on private education,
the other one not.

At the heart of parenting lie your core values and
attitudes. Start by clarifying the values that are
most important to you. What kind of parent do
you want to be? What atmosphere do you want
your children to grow up in? The key is to embody
these qualities yourself so that you are an inspiring
role model. If you want your children to be happy
and healthy, prioritise your own wellbeing. If you
want them to be optimistic about life, make sure
that you look on the bright side. Blend your
strengths with those of your partner to give your
children the best of both worlds.

TIP

The greatest gift you can give a child
is unconditional love.

59

Sex never stops –
it just changes

'At the beginning of our relationship we were
like rabbits, couldn't stop. Now we're lucky to
make love once a month.' It's a common story in
a long-term relationship. Coming to terms with
how sex changes is crucial because making love
plays an important part in keeping your
relationship alive.

Allow sex to deepen your levels of intimacy, love and understanding. Make sure that you put in the effort. It's all too easy to let sex take a back seat. Continue to be romantic and stay attractive for each other. Dress in a style that appeals. Wear scents that arouse passion. Most importantly, meet each other's needs. There is a joke that women fake orgasm because men fake foreplay. A loving relationship enables you to be honest about what you both want and not to take sex too seriously. Retaining a sense of humour, especially when you're tired and the 'to do' list is full, is an essential element of great sex.

TIP

Let sex be an expression of your love

60

Put toothpaste on your partner's brush, even when you don't want to!

Every night I go into the bathroom and either find my toothbrush with toothpaste already squeezed on to it or I leave Veronica's ready to use. We do this even when we don't want to! It's important to have rituals in your relationship that show how much you care. These are little ways of saying

'I love you', which you should continue to do even if you have had a fight. In fact they are a great way of breaking through any lingering resistance if an upset has occurred.

Performing a ritual means that you have to get off your high horse. It is an act of surrender that helps to restore love to the relationship. One couple I knew always had a kiss before dinner. Whatever state they were in, whatever they had to do, they made a point of consciously connecting before getting on with their lives. Ensure that you have some rituals in your relationship which demonstrate your love and affection.

TIP

Create a ritual that demonstrates
your love and commit to it

61

End comparisons

Have you ever found yourself singing the praises of your ex, reminiscing about how gorgeous he/she was and how much fun you'd had?

It's funny how we can suffer from moments of amnesia and, for instance, start comparing our partner to an ex – and the ex comes up trumps.

Comparing one person to another, or one experience to another, never works because everyone and everything is unique.

If you notice yourself in the comparison trap, talk about it with your partner. Explain that you feel it prevents you from being truly present in your relationship and that you want to let it go. Ending comparisons allows you to gain the most from now.

T I P

Focus on the unique qualities of your partner

62

Become a good map reader

We had just bought a second car. Driving home, I said that I could use it for work because it was better than our other car. Veronica said that she thought we'd bought it for her. I exclaimed, 'What do you mean, it's your car? I thought that everything we had was shared.' She said that it had been her idea to get another car for when we have our child. We had been heading off in different directions because we had different 'maps', different understandings of what we were doing.

A 'map' is a personal interpretation about what something means. Since we all have different 'maps' we all have different interpretations. Check where your partner is coming from before laying down your 'map'. Ask them, '*How do you see this situation*' in order to gain greater understanding. Sharing the same 'map' will keep your relationship on track.

Your willingness to understand your partner will bring you great rewards

63

Count to three – then walk away

Do you have a habit of getting attracted to another person whilst in a relationship? If so, learn to walk away. It's the result of having a low intimacy threshold, which means that you can only handle so much closeness before pulling away. People often claim that they want greater intimacy, but find that it can feel quite threatening when they experience it.

The way out is to recognise when it happens. It is natural to find other people attractive, but you don't have to act on it. Walk away from the situation and discuss your feelings with your partner for the purpose of letting them go. Don't use this condition to take away from your relationship. The more you can let yourself become intimate, the more you will let your relationship flourish. Make sure that you leave your fear of intimacy behind rather than leaving your relationship.

TIP

Break through the fear of intimacy and reach greater vitality and fun

64

Expect the unexpected

Here is one money-back guarantee for a relationship – it is going to change. Therefore the quicker you get used to the idea the more you will be able to rise to the challenge.

There are four main stages which it is helpful to recognise:

1. The honeymoon stage – when your partner can do no wrong and they are the apple of your eye.

2. The disillusionment stage – when your partner falls off their pedestal and the dream seems to have shattered.

3. The misery stage – when you appear to have hit a brick wall and you feel victimised by the relationship. Communication has ceased and deadness ensues.

4. The miracle stage – when you both take responsibility for the relationship and you experience mutual respect and unconditional love.

Remember: a relationship can go through these stages in a day, or a lifetime. Be flexible and willing to surf the waves of change.

T I P

Change is inevitable, get used to it

65

Be adventurous – walk down a different street

Do you remember the film *Groundhog Day*? Bill Murray finds himself caught in a time loop in which every day is the same as the last. Our relationship can turn into a monotonous routine unless we are willing to make new choices. Notice if you have any repetitive issues in your relationship. For example, do you tend to struggle with money, or with time? Do you have a habit of feeling a victim? Is there a continuous theme of competition and one-upmanship? If so, it's time to take a new route.

Discuss with your partner those areas where you feel stuck in a rut. Look at new choices that you can make together which will bring you different outcomes. In order to experience a change it takes a small amount of 'how to' and a large amount of 'want to' – your willingness is the key.

T I P

Do something different and you'll
get something different

66

Check:
fear or fact

I used to fear that Veronica would leave me. I
had suffered loss in previous relationships and
found it difficult to trust. I had to keep checking
it out with her until I finally realised that it was
simply an unfounded fear, not a fact.

Probably the greatest obstacle to enjoying a
loving relationship is fear. Fear is at the root of
every problem, every pain and every drama.

Fear masks itself in various ways. It tricks you into believing that it's good for you. It makes out that it protects your best interests and that it knows best. All that fear really does is limit your experience.

Before following your fear, check it out. Remember this – a fear is often *false* *evidence* *appearing* *real*. Once you discover that your fear is not a fact, you are free to love fully.

T I P

Giving up fear is a gateway to
new levels of freedom

67

Give 'em enough rope

I met a woman who was happily married to her husband – who lived in a different house! It seemed a strange concept but it apparently worked for them. They enjoyed having their own space and consciously deciding when they saw each other. I'm not suggesting that you give your partner breathing room so literally, but it is important to be happy spending time apart.

Some couples go on different holidays in order to pursue their own interests. Others socialise or pursue hobbies on their own. Be clear about how much time you plan to be apart. This ensures that you get the right balance and adds to your appreciation of each other. If you do feel reluctant to give 'em enough rope, commit to trusting more and worrying less.

TIP

Appropriate absence makes the
heart grow fonder

68

Take a stand

Who are you in your relationship? I had a client who complained that he had a tendency to lose himself in his relationship. He was unable to follow through on his wishes and he would land up passively agreeing with his girlfriend. These are symptoms of being compliant – a condition that means you sacrifice yourself in your relationship.

To see if you suffer from it read on:

1. Do you assume responsibility for your partner?

2. Do you have difficulty expressing feelings?

3. Do you worry how your partner may respond to your opinions?

4. Do you find it difficult to make decisions?

The catch with being compliant is that although it may look like you are being caring and loving, you fall into a pattern of being 'used' by your partner. Learn to stand up for yourself. Explain to your partner the habit of compliance and your decision to break it. It will deepen their respect for you.

Decide what you want and go for it

69

Make sure what's important stays important

We live in a busy world. In this hurried existence it is easy to forget what is really important. For instance, doing the washing up is a worthwhile act, but is it really more important than having a cuddle? Going to the pub with friends is fun, but is it really more important than having quality time together?

Probably the biggest trap today is putting work ahead of a relationship. Although work is very important, what price are you willing to pay? Are you prepared to sacrifice your relationship in the name of success? Ask yourself, '*What is important to me?*' Is it friendship? Fun? Sharing? Security? Love? Sex? A relationship needs attention. Make sure that you prioritise what's most important.

TIP

Decide what's most important
to you in your relationship
and put it first

70

The boomerang effect

One of the biggest questions I get asked is, 'How do you know if a relationship is right?' My favourite response is 'try and get rid of it and see if it comes back to you!' Believe me. If a relationship has a future, no matter how many mountains you climb, rivers you swim and swamps you have to wade through, there will always be a way forward.

I have witnessed countless relationships where
one or both parties have done everything to try
and end the relationship. Affairs, divorce and
even leaving the country. Yet if the love is there
it will continue to come through.

TIP

Trust in the strength
that lies in your relationship

71

Don't edit
yourself out

'He/she is not going to be interested in you.'
'You're not good enough.' 'You can't say that.'
'You can't go out looking like that.' Sound
familiar? There is a voice in your head that
doesn't stop judging you. Known as *The Critic*,
it has a habit of preventing you from being more
honest, more real, more loving and more
adventurous.

The Critic is something you have learned. It is not natural to you. It means that you beat yourself up, give yourself a hard time and generally play small. Would you be willing to let go of *The Critic*? Would you be willing to give yourself a wider brief? Decide to make *The Critic* redundant and remind yourself that you are okay. As you do so you will discover new levels of confidence, creativity and joy.

T I P

Remind yourself that who you are
makes a difference

72

Upgrade your software

Unless you have recently been overhauled, you could be operating on a faulty mechanism. Family and friends can influence you in unhelpful ways, leading you to forget what actually works for you.

Now is the time to update your information. Become aware of any beliefs that are holding you back. For example; 'Relationships are difficult',

'They never work out', 'You can't trust anyone'. Once identified, you need to erase the belief and send it to the wastebasket. You now have a clear space in which to create a new belief. Entertain possibilities such as; 'My relationships work out for the best for all concerned' and 'By trusting myself I can trust others'. Click save and add these to your documents. You can open these documents whenever you choose until these possibilities become your new beliefs.

Find your freedom through being able to choose new beliefs

73

Invest wisely

Sometimes a relationship breaks down and you don't know why. The mystery of what makes a relationship work can sometimes seem unfathomable.

In order not to lose an important relationship it's essential to build up large amounts of trust. In his bestseller, *The Seven Habits of Highly Effective People*, Stephen Covey uses the metaphor of an Emotional Bank Account to describe how much trust exists.

Deposits are made through behaviour such as listening, loving, honesty and having integrity. This builds trust and safety against which you can make withdrawals. A withdrawal is behaviour such as making a mistake or unclear communication. When your trust account is high you have flexibility and understanding in relation to your withdrawals. If you have gone into the red through the habit of being short, sharp and bad-tempered then you will have nothing to draw upon. Battles can ensue and your relationship can be destroyed.

TIP

Never miss an opportunity to build trust in your relationship

74

Take position number 3

How do you look at a problem in your relationship when it appears overwhelming? I suggest that in moments of need you could do worse than seeing your relationship from three different positions.

1. Your own. Looking at your relationship through your own eyes.

2. Your partner's. Looking at your relationship through their eyes.

3. An observer's. Looking at your relationship as if you were a fly on the wall.

You use your own position when you want
to pursue your own interest. However, if you
occupy only this position then you become
selfish. You use your partner's position when
you want to understand them more. But if you
occupy only this position then you can lose
yourself and become compliant.

Taking position number 3 enables you to see
what is happening. It gives you a sense of
objectivity and perspective. Use position number
3 to move to a 'time out' place where you can
take stock of a problem and gain new insights
which benefit your relationship.

T I P

Become the observer of your own
relationship

75

Focus on fun

Woody Allen once said, '*Most of the time I have no fun, the rest of the time I have no fun at all!*' If this sounds like your relationship, it's time to ring the changes. Fun is a state of mind. It is a choice to see the humour in situations, to behave in a light-hearted manner and to prioritise play. Don't postpone fun for a Friday night, or a special occasion. See how you can bring the spirit of fun into any situation, including mundane tasks such as housework and grocery shopping.

Let fun wash away your worries. It's hard to worry about things whilst retaining a playful outlook. Ask yourself, '*How much anxiety does it take to solve a problem?*' None, because worry is not a solution for anything. However, fun gives you a choice. It helps you to entertain new possibilities, change your thinking and play with different options.

TIP

laugh, and the whole game changes

76

Get the balance right

Always dashing around? Never have enough time to get things done? Want to be doing three or four things simultaneously? Welcome to modern living. When you're going at such a pace the challenge is to get a healthy balance between your work and other aspects of your life. Failure to do so can turn work into a major cause of stress in your relationship.

Be careful of succumbing to a 'guilt' culture, which refers to the pressure people feel to work long hours, including weekends, forgo holiday leave and miss family commitments. It may look impressive at work to sacrifice your personal life, but there is a price to pay. Your partner can tolerate only so much absence. Make sure that you address your priorities as a partnership. For example, plan how much time you're going to spend together and stick to it as much as possible. Of course, work does sometimes have unpredictable requirements, but if this happens be quick to reset a healthy balance.

TIP

Having a great relationship supports your work and your life

77

Have a firm anchor

When I was younger and performed on the violin I was a bag of nerves before going onto the platform. The only thing that really got me through was remembering to breathe! All my crazy thoughts would drift into the background if I stayed focused on my breath. I realise now that it acted as an anchor that kept me centred and sane.

There are times when you're going to be a bag of nerves in your relationship, when you're going to lose the plot. At these moments it's helpful to have your own anchor, something that pulls you back to what truly matters. You create an anchor by thinking about something that is meaningful for you. It may be a word, a statement, an image or a memory. It needs to have a strong emotional impact on you. For example, if love is important to you, saying the word love could be an anchor. If happiness is important to you, using a memory of when you were most happy might be an anchor. Drop your anchor by focusing on it whenever you feel awash at sea. The more you use it the more helpful it will become.

Before flying off the handle in your relationship focus on what matters

78

Keep your eyes wide open

Relationships are a challenge. As soon as you think you can press cruise control there is another obstacle to overcome. However, there is hope. A solution is at hand. In his bestseller, *The Road Less Travelled*, the psychiatrist Dr Scott Peck opens with the statement, *'Life is difficult'*. He goes on to explain that if we can accept the difficulties in life we cease to have a problem with them.

To apply this theory in a relationship is a wise move. Often we look for solutions through external sources such as marriage, children and finances. They may make a difference but they're not going to sort your problems out once and for all. Marriage is a blessing, but it's not the answer to everlasting happiness. Children are an extraordinary gift, however they bring their own issues. Money may help, but beyond survival increased wealth does not bring increased happiness. Accepting the difficulties a relationship brings means that you can benefit from all your experiences.

TIP

Recognise that difficulties are
opportunities in disguise

79

Share the
winnings

He wants to see a film. She wants to have
dinner. He wants to watch the football. She
wants to watch the documentary. What do you
do? Think win/win. In other words make sure
that you both get what you want. This can be
easier said than done! It requires that you be
prepared to negotiate until you reach an
outcome that works for both of you.

To think win/win requires a flexible mind. It is based on a belief that there is always a solution to any dilemma. To practise this idea think about how you could turn a current win/lose situation into a win/win. What step would you need to take and how would you know if you had reached a win/win? The only way to be sure is to check it out with your partner. Employ this secret and watch the trust and fun in your relationship increase.

The only way for you to be truly fulfilled is for your partner to be fulfilled too

80

You cannot change the leopard's spots

I was seeing Charles for the first time. His relationship was top of the agenda. Almost immediately he launched into an attack on his partner, pointing out all the traits that she needed to change. He exclaimed that he had tried everything in his power to change her but to no avail.

Dangerous stuff.

When couples try to change each other it is a form of control, trying to manipulate their partner to fit their picture.

Be honest with yourself, and ask yourself, 'Why am I with my partner if I want to change them?' Placing conditions on them, such as: you must dress a certain way, you must have certain interests and you must share similar viewpoints, is not healthy and will only result in your partner resenting you. The fact is that if they want to change they will. Stop trying to change them and change the way you respond to them. Your willingness to see them differently sets you free.

TIP

Your greatest influence on your
partner is your example

81

Assumptions
are a recipe
for disaster

How does it feel to be at the other end of an
assumption? Not so good. Making assumptions
is a symptom of complacency, which is often the
beginning of a slippery downhill path. To assume
is a sign of laziness. It is comparable to saying
'I'm not going to make the effort to listen to you
and to find out what you really want, I'm just

going to make it as convenient for myself
as possible'.

Since we don't always know if we are making
assumptions, the secret is to keep checking in
with your partner. Ask questions that help you
to discover what's happening for them. For
instance, 'Am I meeting your needs?' 'Do you feel
that I understand you?' It is useful to set a
ground rule together that you agree to check
things out. Therefore you don't even assume that
you're not making assumptions!

TIP

You constantly reinvent your
relationship by not making
assumptions

82

Don't take yourself seriously

Do you suffer from a condition of
overseriousness, in which you make mountains
out of molehills and blow problems up out of
proportion? If so it's time to learn to smile at
yourself again. As a young child you possessed a
natural ability to laugh at yourself which may
have got lost over the years. In a relationship
rekindling this spirit is a lifeline since you are
going to make mistakes along the way.

The quickest way to correct human error is to be able to smile at yourself, learn the lesson and move on. When you begin to sweat the small stuff you lose perspective and problems can appear far worse than they really are. Be careful not to get addicted to the drama of endless relationship problems. You are not auditioning for a soap opera! You will enjoy far more satisfaction by transforming your problems with a large dose of humour. Your partner will also be immensely grateful.

TIP

Smile and your partner will
smile too

83

Kindness is a loving medicine

The English novelist Aldous Huxley was once asked to sum up his lifetime's work. He paused for a moment, and then simply said, *'Try to be a little kinder'*.

In a world where we are often encouraged just to look out for ourselves, being kind is not glamorous. However, to apply Huxley's wisdom to a relationship gives you what you want.

Kindness builds trust, understanding and intimacy. It breaks down defensive walls and heals old wounds. One touch of kindness can make your partner's day. A loving word or a thoughtful act can interrupt their daily routine and be a great reminder of how much you care. Be kind for no particular reason; this really catches them unaware and puts a smile in their heart.

TIP

Be unreasonably kind

84

Be the person you want to be with

Mahatma Gandhi declared, '*Be the change you want to see*'. He lived his life by that credo and eventually died because of it. This powerful idea can lead to you being proactive about what you want in your life. Often people fall into the trap of looking for their ideal partner, or wishing their partner would change, claiming that then and only then will they be happy.

The secret is for you to step forward with the personality traits and qualities that you want to attract in someone else. If you want love, become loving. If you want friendship, be a good friend. If you want fun, become fun to be with. You become so much more attractive when you realise that you are a whole person already, and that your happiness is not dependent on somebody else. A relationship transforms if just one person applies this idea. Stop looking outside yourself for the answers and realise that they lie within you.

TIP

Embody the qualities that you want
to see in your partner

85

Go where your heart beats loudest

'My life is full. I don't have space for a relationship. However, I've met this person and my heart has taken over. I'm doing everything I can to resist it but to no avail. My work is suffering, I feel exhausted and I can't think clearly.' A client disclosed their recent dilemma.

What happens when you resist what your heart is telling you? Chaos, disaster, confusion and upset?

It is vital to listen to your 'inner-tuition', your inner voice which knows what is best and right for you. In our high tech world, filled with information, theories and logical thought, 'gut feelings' don't always rank high. However, most people report that they make their major decisions based on intuition. Learn to discern between 'gut feelings' and logical thinking. The decision to follow your heart sets you up for an exciting adventure. You don't know where it will take you but you do know that it will be for the best.

TIP

Your heart knows best

86

Keep breathing!

It was a day that I had never quite believed would happen – my wedding day. As I stood in front of my family and friends I'll never forget the moment when the registrar turned to me and asked if I would take Veronica to be my lawfully wedded wife. I lost my breath. He reminded me to keep breathing and answer the question!

When faced with an intense moment, whether it consists of fear or ecstasy, there is a tendency to hold your breath. This blocks the natural flow of emotion and can make it more difficult to handle. Remind yourself to keep breathing, taking deep breaths into your abdominal area. This will help you to relax and make the most of the moment.

TIP

When confronted, breathe

87

Love is the best revenge

Have you ever plotted a strategy for getting even with a partner? Have you ever withheld your love, shut down communication or been vengeful in your behaviour? If so, welcome to the human being club.

The desire for revenge is one of our most powerful emotions, and we can go to considerable lengths to justify it. However, revenge is not a solution. Whenever you try and even the score by matching your partner's behaviour, for example by having an affair, putting them down or backbiting, you lose out. It might appear to give you temporary satisfaction, but that soon passes and you're left licking your wounds. Keep your heart open and continue loving. Be willing to let go of grievances and see things differently. We all have our side of a story but it is your capacity to genuinely understand your partner's behaviour that will bring you the fulfilment you seek.

TIP

Your commitment to love will ensure your peace of mind

88

Celebrate differences

You feel that you have met your soul mate. You like the same food, watch the same films, listen to the same music and have the same sense of humour. The next week you've split up. This can leave you thinking that if you can't have a long-lasting relationship with someone you have so much in common with, how can you have a great relationship with someone with different tastes and interests?

Although sharing similar interests and tastes can add to compatibility, it is not a prerequisite for a great relationship. In fact, your ability to value differences and see them as strengths is a wise move.

Maybe your partner likes to lie on the couch whereas you like to get up and go. Maybe your partner likes to be very organised whereas you like to leave things lying around. Maybe your partner likes to shop whereas you like to save. Maybe your partner likes comedies whereas you like dramas. Learn to recognise and respect your differences in order to give your relationship room to move.

T I P

Differences add value
and balance a relationship

89

Never, never, never give up

Have you ever run a marathon? If so you know
that there is a point at which you hit 'the wall'
and that if you break through you get a second
wind. Seeing a relationship as a marathon and
not a sprint means that you are in there for the
long run and prepared never to give up. You
start to take care of the little things, leaving no
stone unturned in order to give the relationship
the best possible chance.

If you're single it's important never to give up on the possibility of creating a relationship. Often the point at which you want to give up is the point at which you have a breakthrough to another experience. Ask yourself, '*What would it take for me never to give up on relationships again?*' Remember, whenever you are tempted to give up you are being invited to choose a better way. Commit to choosing love, to choosing help and to choosing peace to reinvent your relationship experience.

T I P

Often the moment at which you
feel like giving up is the moment
when you have a breakthrough

90

Now is the greatest gift

'How are you?' 'We're getting there,' the answer comes back. 'Where are you getting?' 'Oh just there.' Sometimes we get so preoccupied with trying to get somewhere in a relationship that we neglect the adventures along the way. That's a great shame. We can get caught waiting to reach a destination whilst life passes us by.

Recognise that the gifts that you seek are available to you right now. In fact, one of the great spiritual truths is that *now* is the richest moment of your life. If you get too caught up with where you're heading it can lead to false fears. Ask yourself, *'How can I make the most of now? What would make a difference to my relationship now?'* Focusing on *now* ensures that you give attention to the little things that make a big difference.

T I P

Stay focused on the present moment; it's filled with eternal treasures

91

Take the time to make your partner feel special

We had hit a busy patch. I had been on the road presenting seminars and Veronica had deadlines to meet at work. One afternoon she called me, asking if I was going to be home that evening. I immediately felt defensive, as if she was checking up on me. Little did I know! Upon arriving home I walked in to the smell of my favourite food.

Candles were lit around the house and a warm bath awaited me. My suspicions were aroused. What did she want? What was on the agenda? I discovered that her only intention was to make me feel special.

It is a great gift to make your partner feel special. Cooking a delicious meal, taking them to a movie, buying a small gift, giving a massage ensures that they feel the warmth of your love and affection.

TIP

What you give comes back to you multiplied

92

Paint a BIG picture

Dare to dream. Think big. How do you see your ideal relationship? Give your creative imagination free rein to develop an inspiring vision for both of you. It should include your deepest values, goals and dreams. It will act as a compass, guiding you to where you want to go. It will provide a sense of direction when you find yourself in the wilderness.

Think about the type of people that you would like to become. Are you the type of couple that light up a room when you walk in, or when you walk out? What qualities would you like to bring to your family, friends and colleagues? How would you like other people to think of you? Visualise your ideal work and leisure time. What kind of lifestyle would you like to share? Ask yourself, *'What aspects of life am I most passionate about?'* Put them at the centre of your vision and commit to living it.

TIP

let your vision inspire your
relationship

93

Anything
is possible

Each year, as we survive another winter, Veronica
suggests that we take a trip to New Zealand to
visit her family. Each year I pose the same
argument. 'We can't afford it. I haven't got the
time. It's too far to go.' She gently reminds me
that anything is possible if we decide it and plan
it. I'm happy to say that we do go and I have got
better at believing that it is possible.

How would you describe your mentality? Do you posses a 'can-do' or a 'can't-do' outlook? Often one person in a relationship will be the possibility thinker, whereas the other focuses on any evidence against new options. Neither is right or wrong, it depends on what you want to create in your life. I have found that playing with the idea that anything is possible is a liberating experience. Before writing off dreams, stay open long enough to be pleasantly surprised.

T I P

Change 'can't' into 'can'
and 'no' into 'yes' before
making decisions

94

live your life on purpose

One holiday, when Veronica and I were in India, we went searching for our purpose, visiting sacred sites and spiritual teachers. Eventually, feeling battered and bruised, we booked an early flight home. Having looked for the big meaning in life we came away with the realisation that a purpose is something you choose rather than find.

It's a great gift to choose the purpose of your relationship together. For example, if love is important to you, then your purpose may be to love and be loved. If happiness is important to you, then your purpose may be to spread happiness. Living your life on purpose means that you stay on track with what really matters to you and adds another dimension to your relationship.

T I P

Let your purpose guide your choices
and actions

95

Arguments are natural

I used to be terrified of arguing. I was convinced
that it meant a relationship was doomed and
that it would come to an irrevocable end.
Thankfully Veronica has a different perspective.
For her an argument simply means having a
disagreement which you then resolve. It involves
no big deal and no dramatic conclusions. As a
result I have learned that it is possible to have an
argument and then move on.

The inability to argue is comparable to doing your washing but not hanging it out to dry. You both need air time. If an argument does occur, allow yourselves the space to get things off your chest. There can be a temptation to jump in too soon to end a conflict. This usually means that it gets suppressed and comes out later. At a neutral time discuss your strategy for handling arguments. Take responsibility, be prepared to disagree, and be realistic; a relationship is not a bed of roses 24/7.

TIP

Be prepared to disagree and be realistic, arguments will happen

96

Keep dating

What to wear? Where to go? What to do? The early dates in a relationship are filled with anticipation, apprehension and excitement. They are special occasions as both people make an effort to impress. Don't let it slip. It's an important part of a relationship.

Once married, Veronica and I noticed that we seemed to spend less quality time together.

Work, family and friends would take over and our relationship often seemed to be last on the list. We decided to change this pattern by making it a priority and scheduling dates into our diary. We may meet up for a meal, a movie, or just stay home with a video and a takeaway. Would it make a difference in your relationship to reinstall the magic of dating? If so, get your diary out and commit to it now.

T I P

Treat your long-term relationship as a new date

97

Don't be afraid to leave if it is not working

Do you stay or do you go? How long do you put up with the fights, arguments, power struggles and misery? Leaving can be an unnerving prospect to face. But face it you must if you can see no future in your relationship.

It takes total honesty to admit that a relationship is over. Your heart knows because the love has died. The flame has been extinguished and you're operating on autopilot. We often keep a relationship going because we either feel bad about ending it or afraid of being alone. If this is the case ask yourself, *'Would I like someone to stay with me because they feel bad about hurting my feelings?'* The most loving act is to be honest. When you know the writing is on the wall, step forward. Share your feelings, including any fear, confusion, guilt and loss. Any separation is painful. However, the sooner you act on your instincts the sooner you set everyone free.

TIP

An ending can be the gateway to
new beginnings

98

Discover the real issue at hand

'Our relationship has gone off the rails, the love has gone out of it,' a couple admitted to me in their first session. 'The fun and friendship is now a distant memory.' When I asked about their situation it transpired that the husband had been made redundant, they had too many large bills to pay, a house that needed fixing and the demands of two young children!

Sometimes you can start to think that your relationship is going badly when it's not the relationship, but the surrounding issues that are colouring it. You cannot see the wood for the trees and blame your relationship, as it appears as good an option as any. The catch is that if you continue to hold your relationship to ransom, it may not be able to pay up and therefore you lose it. Learn to distinguish between other issues and your relationship. Prioritise your current concerns and develop a strategy for resolving each one.

TIP

Your relationship can be great
even when life is difficult

99

Be obsessed with the bottom line

In a relationship make your bottom line your core values. Being passionate about what is most important to you ensures that you live your life on purpose. Take some quiet time with your partner to discuss your deepest values. They will probably include things such as: love, happiness, health, family, fun and contribution.

Once identified, write a statement of intent that expresses your commitment to how you want to live. For example; *'We choose to have a loving, fun relationship, which has honesty and understanding at its heart. We commit to communicating fully, forgiving fast and being compassionate. We appreciate one another and value each other's differences.'*

Let your statement become the rock that you always come back to whenever you find yourself drifting off to sea.

T I P

Your core values guide your relationship choices

100

Reveal secrets fast!

The biggest secret is not to keep secrets! The more that you let other people know what you have learned, the more relationship success you will enjoy. Give this book to your partner, to your friends, or to someone you're attracted to. Each time you share a secret with someone, you reinforce the message for yourself.

We all need constant reminders. In our busy lives it's easy to forget the essential nuggets of truth. By practising *The Secrets*, your relationship will continue to grow in the direction that you want. Imagine putting as much commitment, dedication and effort into your relationship as you probably put into your work. You would reap the benefits in a short space of time.

T I P

Share *The Secrets* with your friends

About the Author

Ben Renshaw is Britain's leading relationship expert, as seen on the UK Channel 4 documentary *Perfect Match*. He is an inspirational speaker, seminar leader, success coach and broadcaster. He travels the world, coaching leaders in business, health and education. He also gives public talks and workshops through The Happiness Project and the Coaching Success Partnership. He is the highly acclaimed author of *Successful But Something Missing* and *Together But Something Missing*, and lives in London with his wife Veronica.

For further information on the work of Ben Renshaw and private coaching sessions contact:

Ben Renshaw
Clifton Gate
Clifton Avenue
London W12 9DR
Tel/fax: 020 8762 0176
E-mail: info@benrenshaw.com
Web site: www.happiness.co.uk

For further information about:

1. The Relationship Intelligence Workshop
2. Coaching Success Training Programme
3. Happiness NOW – the 8-Week Happiness
   Programme
4. Coaching Happiness – The Certificate Training
   for Trainers
5. Books and Tapes
6. Coaching Success Corporate Seminars

please contact:

The Happiness Project
Elms Court
Chapel Way
Oxford OX2 9LP
Tel: 01865 244414
Fax: 01865 248825
E-mail: hello@happiness.co.uk
Web site: www.happiness.co.uk

The Secrets Library

Carlson, Richard. *Don't Sweat the Small Stuff in Love*. Hodder & Stoughton, 1999

Chopra, Deepak. *The Path To Love*. Rider Books, 1997

Covey, Stephen. *The 7 Habits of Highly Effective People*. Simon & Schuster, 1989

Cox, Tracey. *Hot Relationships*. Corgi Books, 1999

Dyer, Wayne. *Your Sacred Self*. Harper Collins, 1995

Holden, Robert. *Shift Happens!* Hodder & Stoughton, 2000

Holden, Robert. *Happiness NOW!* Hodder & Stoughton, 1998

Holden, Miranda. *Relationships and Enlightenment*. THP, 1997

Jeffers, Susan. *Feel the Fear and Do It Anyway*. Rider, 1991

McGraw, Phillip C. *Relationship Rescue*. Vermilion, 2000

Peck, Scott. *The Road Less Travelled*. Rider, 1978

Williamson, Marianne. *A Return to Love*. Thorsons, 1992

Wilson, Paul. *Calm for Life*. Penguin, 2000